121 Tips

on Raising a Child of Color

AN EASY-READING, MOTIVATIONAL MIX OF SUPER
SUGGESTIONS FOR CHILD-REARING SUCCESS!

Larry Mansfield Robbins, BA, M.Ed.
&
Dr. Juneau Kipola Robbins

Beaver's Pond Press, Inc.
Edina, Minnesota

ISBN 1-890676-66-7

Library of Congress Catalog Number: 00-105354

Printed in the United States of America.

03 02 01 00   5 4 3 2 1

Dedicated to every human being

Regardless of race, creed or color

Finding commitment within themselves

To take the place of an absentee parent.

Thank you

121 TIPS ON RAISING A CHILD OF COLOR

"Within the mindset and dedication of a child's guardian lies the rise or fall of a nation."

—Dr. Juneau Kipola Robbins

THE CHALLENGE OF RAISING A CHILD OF COLOR; the image immediately conjures distinctly different images in the minds of people the world over. Struggle, admiration and respect, or fear, loathing and laziness. Whatever your opinion, children of color, be they Black, Hispanic, or any other non-white race, are suffering. The time is ripe for parents of "minority" children to re-dedicate themselves to proficient parenting, thereby raising the standard of our rising minority nation.

Like crops left unharvested in a farmer's field, left to stand long into the fall season, the life-potential of many children of color is withering. Morals are misplaced at a time when HIV infection is epidemic amongst our youth. Love is lacking at a time when young people need to learn, and live, love the most. Guidance and discipline have become the responsibility of society at a time when they need be taught at home. Self-preservation and self-satisfaction have become the order of the day...but all is not lost.

When a farmer's crop is left to stand long into the fall season, long after the peak of its potential has expired, that crop slowly begins to decompose, die, and fall to the ground. With the passing of time, those same soil-ridden, decaying crops begin to act as fertilizer, energizing and vitalizing the nutrient-depleted soil. The following year that same soil gives rise to a new generation of *super crops*', sprouting taller, stronger and more bountiful than before. *Rotten regenerates to ripe.*

The same concept can hold true for the world's children of color, regardless of social or economic situation. Our children of today, impressionable and innocent, will become the leaders of tomorrow. Future leaders need the support of a solid foundation; morally, socially, spiritually, economically and intellectually. The followers of tomorrow will need the same solid foundation, lest they easily be lead astray. It is a guardian's responsibility to give birth to this foundation.

121 Tips on Raising a Child of Color contains simple, but powerful, parenting advice intended to help create such a foundation. **DO NOT LET THE SIMPLICITY OF THE WORDS FOOL YOU!**

GETTING THE MOST FROM YOUR EFFORT

HOW TO BEST READ
121 TIPS ON RAISING A CHILD OF COLOR

Depending on your purpose for reading this book, whether purchased in a store or received as a gift, the manner in which you read the following pages will determine what you take from your effort.

The greatest beauty of an idea is its indestructibility. Ideas are powerful. Ideas are forever. Ideas ignite the thought process that leads to self-evolution and self-improvement. *121 Tips on Raising a Child of Color* is packed full of time-tested, practically proven ideas for child-rearing success. It is the first book of its kind written specifically for parents of color, regardless of race, creed or ethnicity.

121 Tips on Raising a Child of Color contains ideas, suggestions and questions. The questions contained within are specifically designed to help you, the reader, focus on suggested parenting advice. It is the questions we ask ourselves, every morning, noon and night, that leads to situation-changing answers in our lives. Simply stated, the more you focus on questions regarding improvement of your parenting skills, the better your brain will naturally develop solutions. Successful parenting, like the development of your thoughts, is a process.

For best results from this book, read the parenting tips aloud. Repeat the same tip several times, forcing the suggestion into your short-term memory. Advice truly meant for *you* will naturally ingrain itself into your long-term memory. After repeating a tip several times, answer the corresponding question. Think on it! Take your time. Hurried answers will not be as valuable as well-thought responses. Write your answers in a journal or diary, or take notes in the space provided at the end of the book. This will allow you to periodically reflect back on your answers, and motivate you to keep moving forward. Share your favorite tips and questions with others!

Ultimately, *121 Tips on Raising a Child of Color* can be read in any manner you choose. Whether you decide to thumb through the pages at random, use the quotes for inspiration, or implement the above-suggested reading system, have fun! Raising a child is the most challenging, rewarding, and important undertaking of your life. Read, learn and enjoy.

1

Let love for your child re-prioritize your priorities. Loving your child and being a good parent is priority #1!

In what ways do I need to re-prioritize my goals in life to make sure my child is at the top of my list?

2

As a child thinks in their heart, so will they become. Instill in your child a strong sense of belief-in-self daily.

What is one specific action I can take today that will help foster self-confidence in my child?

3

Regard your child as the best they can be,
and chances are excellent they will become
the best they can be.

When I look at my child what do I see?
Do I see a curious, learning,
well-adjusted individual?

4

Do not be afraid to let your child know when you don't know. You will not lose credibility by being honest.

*Am I always honest with my child,
or do I tend to disguise the truth for
the sake of convenience?*

5

Admit your mistakes. Your child will respect you rather than be upset with you for being stubborn in your ways!

*When I am wrong about something,
do I allow pride to prevent
me from admitting I am wrong?*

6

Always say what you mean and mean what you say. Never make a threat, claim or promise you will not keep.

When my child violates the rules of our home, do I pass punishment, or do I look the other way?

Create a feeling of cultural pride in your home by exposing your child to ethnic art, history and literature.

Where is the closest bookstore to my home that specializes in ethnic art, history and culture?

8

If a lesson in tough love is what your child needs, give it to them. Tough love is a greater love than soft love.

When I punish my child for willful disobedience, are my actions just and concretely understood?

9

Consider your child the perfect,
personalized package from God, then treat
your child accordingly.

Have I taken time today to thank God for blessing me with such a wonderful creation?

10

Seek the knowledge of your peers; tap the wisdom of your elders. Parents have existed since the dawn of mankind.

*Who are three individuals I admire,
having raised children before me,
that I can use as resources?*

11

Compliment and cooperate with your child.
Don't constantly criticize and condemn.
Build them up!

*What is one specific thing my child did
today, no matter how small,
that I can compliment them for?*

Adopt the attitude that raising your child is the most fabulous, fun and fulfilling feeling of your life!

What is the most recent wondrous thing my child has done that brings a smile to my face?

13

Your child knows more than you think. Talk to your child candidly about drugs before you feel they are ready.

Where can I find resources to help me talk to my child about drugs as easily and effectively as possible?

14

Your child knows more than you think. Talk to your child candidly about sex before you feel they are ready.

Where can I find resources to help me talk to my child about sex as easily and effectively as possible?

15

Children mimic what they see, not what they are told. Your child's actions reflect their environment.

*Does my everyday lifestyle
reflect the behavior I want my child
growing-up to exhibit?*

16

When your child does wrong, make sure they understand what about their actions was wrong. Take time to explain.

Do I chastise my child without explanation, or do I explain to them why their actions were wrong?

17

Take pride in your child's appearance.
Clean, tidy clothing and good hygiene are
inexpensive yet priceless.

Do I provide my child with fresh, clean clothing and the bathing and brushing tools they require?

18

Practice, preach, train and teach proper washing and grooming techniques necessary for good hygiene.

*Have I taught my child
everything they need to know about
personal grooming and hygiene?*

19

Expose your child to many different cultures from a very young age. Ignorance is the primary root of prejudice.

Have I made an honest, conscious effort to expose my child to unfamiliar races, places and cultures?

20

Instill in your child the golden rule that children are not permitted to infringe upon the rights of others.

Have I actively taught my child to respect the rights of all people, regardless of race, creed or ethnicity?

21

Put a dollar a day away for your child everyday of their life, then give them the lump sum for their 18th birthday.

Am I adding at least seven dollars a week to my child's savings to help them get started in life?

22

Praise and encourage your child sincerely and often. Look for the good in your child and you will find it.

*What are the qualities and attributes
I admire, and am most proud of,
in my child?*

23

Education is a passport past poverty. Get involved in your child's schooling; volunteer at least one day a month.

What learning activities are my child involved in where my input can make a direct difference?

24

Your child needs to spend a lot of time with you, not just quality time.
MAKE time to spend with your child.

Do I spend as much time as possible with my child, or do I allow work and play to take time away?

25

Forget yesterday's mistakes in raising your child; today is a brand new day. Pledge progress from this day forth.

What have I learned from yesterday's experiences that makes me a better parent today?

26

God was the perfect parent, yet Adam and Eve sinned. Do not dwell in guilt over your child's mistakes.

*Do I forgive myself daily
for the transgressions of my child,
or do I harbor guilt deep within?*

27

In order to raise a moral and mannerly child you must first become a parent whose manners are moral.

Do I live a morally sound and upright lifestyle, or are my actions and lifestyle degrading?

28

Joke and play with your child
enough to keep life fun, but not enough to
teach the persistent pursuit of pleasure.

*What is one memorable moment
shared between my child and I
that makes me laugh aloud?*

29

The easiest, most effective way to change your child's behavior is to change your behavior toward your child.

What can I change about my behavior that would allow me to communicate better with my child?

30

Confronting a problem does not guaranty a
solution, but no solution is possible unless
a problem is first confronted.

What action can I take today
to confront the most
plaguing problem in my child's life?

31

Children learn faster, better and more accurately under a spirit of approval versus the spirits of abuse and blame.

What kind of environment do I promote for my child as they learn about the ways of the world?

The greater example of excellence set for a child, the less a parent will need to enforce the rules of the home.

In what ways do I, and others involved in my life, set elevated examples of excellence for my child?

The lessons of childhood become the instincts of adulthood. Teach your child their life-lessons well.

What are the toughest life-lessons
my child needs to know
before they forge forth on their own?

34

A child who identifies learning with love will grow to love learning. Take time to read with your child.

What story, book or article can I read and talk about with my child today, in the spirit of love?

35

Enlighten your child to the principles of Kwanzaa early, then live the principles of Kwanzaa 365 days a year.

Do I know the principles of Kwanzaa well enough to teach them, live them and share them with my child?

36

The first six years of a child's life are more important to a child's success than four years of college. Make time!

*Have I created a solid enough
foundation in my child's youngest years
to prepare them for life?*

37

Your child hears everything you say. Every conversation, prayer, argument and joke. Walk and talk accordingly!

*Is my everyday language and conduct
the type of language and conduct
that I expect from my child?*

38

Knowledge in, knowledge out. Truth in, truth out. Garbage in, garbage out. Input equals output.

*What kind of television programs,
musical lyrics and reading materials
do I condone for my child?*

39

Guarantee your child gets plenty of physical exercise. Active children learn, play and grow much better.

What kind of physical activities do I encourage for my child? What activities does my child enjoy the most?

40

The daily motivation of a good parent is love, not money, luxury or career. Children need to be loved.

*When I wake-up every morning
and think of my child, do I think
of the love I have for them?*

41

Say "NO" to activities that unnecessarily take time away from irreplaceable time spent with your child.

88

*Do I place my child foremost
in my life, or do I allow work
or social things to come first?*

42

The most important thing a father can do for his child is love their mother, regardless of the parents' relationship.

*Do I express love and respect
for my child's other parent, or do I allow
negativity to surface?*

43

Be authoritative, but patient, with your child. Children learn something new every single day.

When my child attempts something new, am I as patient and supportive as I can be?

44

Children who help around the house will help outside the house, making them of greater value to the world.

*What are the daily, weekly
and monthly chores I set for my child?
How do I reward them?*

Keep materials relating to ethnic
and cultural heroes around your home.
Discuss them often with your child.

Who are the heroes of my heritage that I admire most? How can I pass their message on to my child?

46

Direct your child firmly, but carefully. Firm direction properly voiced is a potent, powerful and promising tool.

*When my child pleads for something
not in their best interest,
do I have the strength to say NO?*

47

Teach your child to say please and thank you.
Courtesy will contribute greatly
to their success.

Are please and thank you routinely heard in the daily communications of my home.

48

Anger is one letter short of danger. Learn to become upset with your child's deeds, not upset with your child.

Do I consciously separate my child's actions from my child when they do something that upsets me?

49

Be proud of your child. Show your pride
every single day. A parent's pride goes a long
way in building self-esteem.

Does my child know how proud I am of them? How can I express my pride daily?

50

Hug your child warmly every morning, noon and night. Hug them once, twice, three times, then hug them again

*How many times have I hugged
my child today? How many times
has my child hugged me?*

51

Envision your child a winner! Create a
powerful self-fulfilling prophecy of
well-being for your child.

*Have I empowered my child fully
by envisioning them to accomplish
all they set out to do?*

52

Mistakes are necessary. Work with your child, encourage your child, to turn their mistakes into successes.

*When my child makes a mistake;
do I chastise them, or do I
encourage them to learn and grow?*

53

Help your child learn from their mistakes by focusing on what they could do next time to get a better result.

*What are three specific ways I
can encourage my child to
learn and grow from their mistakes?*

54

A parent is like a shepherd; a child is like a lamb in need of a good shepherd. Guide and guard your flock.

Am I leading, guiding and guarding my child down the proper paths to the best of my ability?

55

Repetition is the creator of character. Often repeated thoughts will become the essence of your child.

What are three positive thoughts my child should think frequently so they become thoughts of habit?

56

Instill in your child a strong sense of spiritual, family and financial values. Place God before family before money.

Do I place God before family, before money, so I may pass this belief system on to my child?

57

Practice a family diet filled with fresh fruit. Fresh fruit will provide many of the nutrients necessary for life.

When I look inside my refrigerator,
or on my kitchen counter, do I
see fresh fruit and vegetables?

58

Wake up every morning full of energy and excitement. Think winning thoughts, then take winning action.

What are three things I am grateful for
that place me in a positive
state of mind, instantly?

59

Do your best to send your child into each day with a positive attitude. Praise them for every little success.

*What compliment can I give my
child today that will help foster feelings
of goodness and grace?*

60

Create at least three daily affirmations that apply directly to you and your child. Repeat them daily.

Where can I place my daily affirmations so my child and I will see them regularly?

61

The chances of a positive, drug-free parent
raising a positive, drug-free child
are wonderful.

*Am I truly setting the best example
a parent can set for my child?
Or do I have some correcting to do?*

62

Teach your child the power of choice.
Different choices have different
consequences, either good or bad.

Have I truly taken the time,
and made an honest effort
to teach my child right from wrong?

63

Tell your child tales of cultural achievement. Let them know they are heirs to a legacy of great triumph.

If I asked my child today to tell a tale of their cultural heritage, how would they respond?

Share goals with your child.
With encouragement and love, they will
develop their own goals as they grow.

*Does my child know their daily,
weekly and monthly goals for the next year?
What are my goals?*

65

Support and encourage your child's career goals. At the same time, insist your child get a solid education.

Does my child understand the importance of having a serious back-up plan in addition to their dream?

66

Look forward in hope, not backward in despair. Constant hope in the future builds power in the present.

What blessings do I have to look forward to in the next day, week, month and year?

67

Give thanks aloud with your child before meals. This will help teach your child an attitude of gratitude.

What is my child's opinion of God?
Do I set a positive example by practicing
my spiritual beliefs daily?

68

Mealtime is the perfect time for sharing, talking and enjoying. Eat with your child as often as possible.

Does my family strive as often as possible to share and replenish ourselves together?

69

Look your child in their eyes when you talk to them. This will help build their sense of self-image and self-worth.

144

When my child talks to me, do I look them in their eyes, or do I tend to look away?

70

When your child knows they are important to you, they will listen to the advice you have to give.

What is one action I can take today to let my child know how precious and important they are to me?

71

Walk together, talk together; in time your child will share their heart. When they do, listen wholeheartedly.

148

*Is there a place near my home
where my child and I can
walk and talk together in peace?*

72

It is better for your child to do their homework while not watching television or listening to the radio.

If television and music helped children learn better, wouldn't schools play them during class?

73

Good study habits developed at a young age will make a tremendous difference later in your child's education.

Do I direct my child's study habits so they are efficient and effective for future learning?

74

Making time to spend with your child is an
investment that will pay uncountable,
lifelong returns.

Do I MAKE enough time to spend with my child, or does my child come second to work, pleasure or play?

75

Forgive yourself. Forgive your child. Forgive everyone else. Forgiveness allows you to fly forward fast and free.

Is my life burdened with anger and resentment, or do I forgive those who trespass against me?

76

Discuss items relating to heritage
with your child. Let those items
inspire excellence.

What is one item relating to heritage that will inspire my child toward great achievement?

77

A child left undisciplined in his own little world will be harshly disciplined by the larger world outside.

Would I prefer to be strict with my child today, or prefer society to be strict with my child tomorrow?

78

Help your child, even when they are of little help to you. This opens the door for them to help you in the future.

*Do I love my child enough
to help them through thick and thin,
regardless of how little they help me?*

79

Show firmness in the disciplining of your child, especially following deliberate acts of defiance.

*Is my firmness tempered with love
and justice in the disciplining of my child?*

80

Keep cool! Don't lose your temper. Your child needs to see how things resolve better when people stay cool.

*Do I allow emotions to dictate my actions,
or are my actions
governed by intellectual decision?*

81

Even children need to nourish their spirit
for total self-fulfillment.
Show your child that God is the way.

Is my child learning to worship and strive for spiritual peace at a pace they understand?

82

You are your child's parent,
not playmate. Maintain your parenting
pedestal. Maintain your authority.

*Do I allow the natural desire
for friendship with my child to influence
my parenting decisions?*

83

When your child willfully does wrong,
punish them. But make sure they
understand why they are being punished.

*Do I take time to explain
to my child the reason for their punishment,
or do I simply punish them?*

84

Real love demands you do what is best
for your child, not what is easy
and convenient for yourself.

Do I possess the courage and strength to make difficult decisions for myself and my child?

85

Love is the Alpha and Omega
of raising a child. Simply love your child.
Love will do what nothing else can do.

Next to the love I feel for God, is love for my child a top priority in my life?

86

A dirty mouth favors dirty thoughts
and future foul language. Do not speak
obscenities before your child.

Does my daily language include obscenities or immoral thoughts in the presence of my child?

87

Actively raise your child in a positive
venue of religion. This will provide growth,
guidance and support.

*Is my "House of Worship" someplace
my child can attend, learn
and share my experience?*

88

Seek inspiration from positive people
and surroundings. Limit your
association with negative people.

*Who are the people in my life
that make me feel low?
How can I limit my association with them?*

89

Understand that you are your child's greatest hero. Think of ways to inspire your child toward magnificence.

What is one action that I can take today to help inspire thoughts of magnificence within my child?

90

Expose your child to positive images of racially unified men and women. Together, unified, in harmony, in love.

*Who are the most unified couples
I know whom I should expose my child to
as often as possible?*

91

The price of success is discipline,
patience and persistence.
The price of failure is anything less.

Do I set a good example for my child by persistently pursuing my goals, or do I give up too easy?

92

Teach your child the concept of
self-responsibility. In life, everyone is
ultimately responsible for themselves.

*Do I allow my child to blame others
for their shortcomings,
or do I teach self-responsibility?*

93

Identify any temptation in your life that may threaten your family. Take action to place temptation in check.

192

What are the temptations in my life that motivate me in a negative manner? How can I remove them?

94

Make time, take time, to spend time alone.
Read, relax and meditate.
This will help shelter your sanity.

Where is my special, quiet place where I can spend time alone, learning, relaxing, evolving?

95

Tell your child, "I love you!" frequently. They should hear it more from you than anyone else.

When is the last time I told my child,
"I love you!"
Has your child heard it from you today?

96

Instill in your child the fact that
no one in the world will do as much for
them as they can do for themselves.

*Does my child understand the concept
of reaping rewards from
seeds previously sown?*

97

Teach your child to respect and protect the elderly. Old and young people have great gifts to offer one another.

*What great wisdom and knowledge
do the elderly possess; ready
to pass on to my child?*

98

Resolve to practice what you preach.
Your child is watching and
observing your behavior.

In my life, do I honestly practice what I preach to the best of my ability.

99

Encourage your child to go the extra mile.
Amazing individuals are developed,
not born. Lead by example.

*Do I make a habit of putting forth
an extra effort in life, or do I settle for less?*

100

Laugh hard and often with your child. Laughter is the best medicine and most efficient form of bonding.

What can I say, or do,
right now that would have my child and I
rolling on the floor in laughter?

101

Don't search for excuses to justify your shortcomings as a parent. There are no excuses for poor parenting.

Do I ever find excuses why I cannot do something for my child that I should do as a responsible parent?

102

Network with other parents.
Develop a rapport with them and share
parenting tips.

Who are my peers that I respect greatly as parents? How can we share parenting skills with each other?

103

Teach your child that people of common ancestry speak in different ways, and there are many different cultures.

Has my child developed an appreciation of their culture, and a healthy respect for other cultures?

104

Teach your child it is better to swallow
pride and walk away from a fight
rather than risk losing their life.

*Do I stubbornly refuse to back down
in a moment of conflict?
What has my child learned from me?*

105

Teach your child a special place
exists inside them which is sacred, spiritual
and Godly. Teach them love.

Do I know the special place inside me that is sacred, spiritual and dedicated to God?

106

Do not teach your child to hate any race or ethnic group. Hate is consuming, weakening and destructive.

When confronted by challenging racial situations, how do I react?

107

Be cognizant of your child's fears, great and small. Help your child to conquer their fears.

How do I feel when I am afraid?
What do I feel when someone
helps me conquer my fears?

108

Using examples from history,
teach your child how minor changes can
multiply to produce major change.

*What are some of the minor changes
I've made in my life that have
resulted in major growth?*

109

Listen patiently to your
child's problems; they are depending on you
for help. Do not disappoint them.

*When my child comes to me with a problem,
do I take time to listen?*

110

A child should walk, talk and behave
as a child. As a parent, you must act
in a manner more mature.

Am I still behaving as I behaved when I was a child, or has my behavior matured?

It is not enough to simply feel love
for your child; you must express your love
through action everyday.

What action can I take every single day to show my child how much I love them?

Learn the art of self-love.
Self-love is the basis for all that is
beautiful, true and meaningful in life.

Have I learned to love myself unconditionally? Is my child learning to do the same?

113

Take time to seriously learn about parenting. Read books. Talk to other parents. Talk to your parents.

Have I spent as much time learning about parenting as I've spent learning less important things?

114

Count slowly to 20 whenever you become
angry with your child. Search for the
love within that calms you.

When my child's actions upset me,
how do I react?
Is my reaction tempered with love?

115

Think to yourself, If this child were me, how would I want to be spoken to? Speak to your child with respect.

*Do I show my child respect
by treating them as the
unique and special individual they are?*

116

Ask your child for their opinion.
Children have opinions, thoughts and ideas.
Let them express!

When is the last time I asked my child for their opinion about something, then acted on it?

117

Frequent ethnic vendors with your child whenever possible. This will help instill a sense of cooperative economics.

240

*How can I better expose my child
to successful ethnic businesses
and the people who run them?*

118

Give your child a loving nickname.
A loving label tells your child they are
precious and extra-special.

*What rare and loving nickname
have I created for my child?
What name has my child given me?*

119

Lighten up! A relaxed and lighthearted
state-of-mind is more natural than
being so somber, strict and serious.

Do I believe the philosophy of not sweating the small stuff, then remembering it's all small stuff?

120

Protect, respect and love all children;
they are all our responsibility.
Truly, it takes a village to raise a child.

*Am I doing all I can to make
a positive impact on all children
I come in contact with?*

121

Ingrain in your child the notion they are tomorrow's leadership. With leadership comes great responsibility.

*What am I doing today
to prepare my child for the
challenge of leadership tomorrow?*

[NOTES]

[NOTES]

To order additional copies of "121 TIPS ON RAISING A CHILD OF COLOR" send a check or money order for $11.95 U.S. (plus $3.00 shipping & handling) to:

Urban Child Publishing
100 South First Street
P.O. Box 583097
Minneapolis, MN 55458-3097

or

Call the toll free **"121 TIPS ON RAISING A CHILD OF COLOR" Hotline** at:
1-877-888-6291

Visit us on the world wide web at:
www.urbanchildpublishing.com

A percentage of all net profits from this book will be donated toward scholarships for children of color. Authors may be contacted through the hotline or website to arrange public appearances and book signings.